LOVECRAFT
COCKTAILS

LOVECRAFT
COCKTAILS

ELIXIRS & LIBATIONS FROM THE LORE
OF H. P. LOVECRAFT

MIKE SLATER

THE COUNTRYMAN PRESS
A DIVISION OF W. W. NORTON & COMPANY
INDEPENDENT PUBLISHERS SINCE 1923

For information about permission to reproduce selections from this book, write to
Permissions, The Countryman Press, 500 Fifth Avenue, New York, NY 10110

For information about special discounts for bulk purchases, please contact
W. W. Norton Special Sales at specialsales@wwnorton.com or 800-233-4830

Manufacturing by Toppan Leefung Pte. Ltd.
Book design by Faceout Studio, Paul Nielsen
Production manager: Devon Zahn

The Countryman Press
www.countrymanpress.com

A division of W. W. Norton & Company, Inc.
500 Fifth Avenue, New York, NY 10110
www.wwnorton.com

978-1-68268-641-6

10 9 8 7 6 5 4 3 2 1

TABLE OF MALCONTENTS

UNCHARTED WATERS

FOREWARNINGS

As the 13 Sacred Bartenders of Leng knew in ancient days now muddled in the depths of thyme . . . *it all starts with the drinks.*

Potions, elixirs, libations—what are they if not cocktails? What do they do, if not attempt to bring us closer to the Numinous, to thin the Veil, and to tune that exquisite gelationous universe between our ears as we attempt to apprehend this nonsense we refer to as "reality"? As H. P. Lovecraft himself put it, "all our respected forbears indulged in the flowing bowl to such an extent as to make fishes seem land animals by comparison." The tradition is as long and storied as . . . stories, so, as any mixologist will do, why not combine them and see what happens? Turn-of-last-century horror literature inspired cocktails? Sure, why not? Fans of our first work of dark culinary delights, *The Necronomnomnom*, are ever-interested in more drinks. The six libations found gracing its pages are never enough. Mere appetizers before the appetizers. When we asked if we should do more drinks, the response was resounding, immediate, and suggestive of insatiable thirst. We shall see, for within the pages of this tome lie more than *six dozen* cocktails inspired by dreaming cities, sunken citadels, mad prophets, necromancers, wizards, monsters, and titans of literature.

This handy (tentacly?) guide is designed to provide the professional and the home party host with an extensive resource for creating a blend (all puns are intended—the books draw power from your screams and laughter . . . I won't say which they prefer . . .) of unique and almost-familiar cocktails sure to appeal to both the casual horror aficionado and the lore-steeped cultist, alike. And for the uninitiated? Oh, you are in for a ride. References abound, should a fragment of text or an image tug at your awareness with unexpected strength— be not surprised. There is much to explore and many an appropriate beverage to accompany your descent into madness.

This work offers a mix (look, I have to keep up the puns or . . . well, let's just leave it at that . . . I *have to* . . .) of both simple variants for busy bartenders and complex concoctions for the refined host or exclusive establishment wishing to offer guests and patrons something exquisitely outré to imbibe. Each is designed to have sensual visual appeal (in the right light, vessel, and configuration of celestial bodies) as well as flavor. Kurt Komoda's haunting illustrations are drawn directly from photographs of the finished cocktails, with all the lavish Lovecraftian flourishes to be expected from Team Necronomnomnom.

Adventurous vendors of victuals and purveyors of liquorous libations will love this book as much as the party host looking to select a few unusual comestibles for discerning guests attending a themed party. For collectors of Lovecraftiana and fans of *The Necronomnomnom*, this tome is meant as a comely companion and diabolical denizen for your liquor cabinets or basement bar.

Seventy-six cocktails ranging from the seductively simple to the fiendishly fancy grace pages designed to be easy to mix from while the sanity-searing art whets the palette of the intended imbiber. Herein you will find powerful spirits bound in lovely liquids. "Do not summon what you cannot put down" never carried more import as sage advice. In fact, it was the last thing one of our test sages said before sliding under the table. Surely, wisdom is wasted on the wise at times . . .

Each drink is drawn from some work of fiction, prose, film, or even the shadowed corridors of the Web Between Worlds. Weird tales of the sort H. P. Lovecraft rose from the grave to become a high priest of dominate here (of course)—but are accompanied by derivations and complimentary modernities that might not exist were it not for him and his contemporaries. What would he think of this tome so inspired by his work, he who said, "Let the graces of wine live in literature?" Nothing good. But then, so many of the man's opinions were so deeply wrong—why should we concern ourselves with them now; and why should his opinion of drink matter in the least? Should you wish to hear it from his desiccated lips, here is an excerpt:

> With so many other destroying agencies at work, liquor may well be classed as a minor evil—and after all, it does not greatly matter whether or not civilisation decays—or at what speed it decays.
>
> In my own family, wine has been banished for three generations[.] Any person with the least character or independence in his voice can manage to be a total abstainer without giving anybody offence or creating any social contretemps.
>
> —H. P. Lovecraft to Zealia Brown Reed, February 13, 1928, *The Spirit of Revision*

Perhaps he could have benefited from a relaxing cocktail . . . or seventy? We cannot know, but we can try them, and engage in wild supposition at great length. In fact, a few of these administered in the proper setting might help. Just be prudent, I advise you. Saying, "Hit me again, Bartender" to something with an uncountable number of night-black tentacles . . . might leave a mark. Enjoy this collection of near-classics and neoclassics as well as the seemingly bonkers ones. Lovecraft refused "to be dictated to by the superficial customs of any age [and] place," so why should our beverages be? Explore responsibly. We want you to return to this plane and these pages with wonder and joy, flavor and fervor. May the speakeasy of things not easily spoken welcome you.

May your vessel always be full
May the hood of your robe conceal all
May you arrive in accordance with prophecy
And may you sip joyfully from the deepest wells of night

Stay thirsty, my fiends.

A WORD ON AUDIENCES

A bar book, which is what this is, is necessarily designed for bars and restaurants as well as home enthusiasts. For this reason, many of the recipes herein are meant to be interesting and elegant variations that are fairly straightforward and easy to prepare. We had to be mindful of the sanity of countless heretofore uninitiated bartenders and mixologists. Several were summoned and subjected to our elixirs, and some were contributed by them. That said, we have clairvoyant cultists and intrepid investigators to please first and foremost. The book is written with you consummate connoisseurs, esoteric entertainers, and eldritch experimenters in mind at all times. You will find appropriately fiddly concoctions strewn through these pages as well. While we hope that you might see some of these in fine establishments that cater to crowds or events thirsty for such things, they were created with the home bar (or laboratory) in mind. Most importantly, the aesthetic of *The Necronomnomnom* has been faithfully preserved, but in a novel format. Liquid rites are, on the whole, less complex—or such a feat would not have been possible. None of this is a stealthy attempt to spread the madness to an ever-widening circle of souls, at all. . . . Nope. Not at all.

In most cases, the listed amounts of components yield enough for a single, generous serving. Exceptions are explicit. In the case of the Old R'lyeh, the shrub you will create is intended to leave enough to put aside for additional indulgences later or for sharing (but you'll need to make more of the main cocktail). It's also wonderful over pork chops, if I may suggest.

A WORD ABOUT BRANDS AND INGREDIENTS

Most brands that are named here are enthusiastically endorsed. Some are my favorites, so I used them during testing because they were on hand. Can you substitute any rum for that rum? Sure you can. Will it be mostly the same? Chances are good. Some brands were used strictly because it helped make a terrible pun work. These can be substituted at will (provided your sense of humor aesthetics allow it). Are any brands really integral to the intended experience of the drink? One or two, but it's your palette—drink what pleases you.

Will There Be a Few Hard-to-Find Ingredients?

Inevitably. Please substitute as creativity or necessity dictates. We have made allowances for your lapses in rigor with the denizens of the Furthest Taverns of Night. You should be fine—should be . . .

Are There Photographs of the Finished Drinks?

I mean, they're all drawings! But, yes, yes, there are photographs—and, yes, you can see them. The Necronomnomnom and this, its firstborn, are spellbooks in aesthetic, but every piece of art is drawn directly from a photograph of the finished item—and we still have those precious originals. I can't say they're of professional quality but they have served the creative process well. You want to see them? Check out The Necronomnomnom on Facebook and Instagram, or email us at TheNecronomnomnomnom@gmail.com. We'll help you out with the Forbidden Images from the Eye of Ph'o'n.

A WORD ON THE SANCTIFIED IMPLEMENTS OF THE TRADE

I started this project with a glass to which the cocktail strainer fit perfectly (or not at all) and a set of measuring cups—I was flying by the seat of my rune-blackened sacramental robes.

My 1930s art deco–style rocket ship cocktail shaker was lost in the void (probably a move), and I could get by without it, right? No, no, not so much. My wife found me a shaker . . . somewhere. Built of solid Indian steel and beautifully decorated with beaten copper wire, it served me well (and stopped me spattering the walls, countertop, and floor with flying gobbets of boozy ichor). It had a "virtue" born of some arcana of physics to do with temperature gradients that I can only dimly guess at: it would seal as if it really did mean to keep those spirits safely locked within *for all time.* My hands are strong. I am The Opener of Jars and Crusher of Cans To Be Recycled in my domain. But this well-sealed shaker nearly did in my aching thumbs and steely digits. Also, the gunshot-like *pop* of it finally releasing and then clanging-like-a-bell into the sink at 1 a.m. gained me no points with my household. Not to mention the obligatory slosh of lost libation that equaled, if more directionally distributed, what had previously escaped through the mismatched glass-and-strainer.

One day, somewhere in the middle of the project, salvation arrived. A mysterious package containing two beautiful shakers of consummate design arrived, unbidden. Had the universe heard my plea? Had it heard the muttered curses of my mate's interrupted slumber? Had the lost spirits consigned to drain down the black stone of sink conveyed to Powers Unknown my plight? Eh, no, it turns out it was Tim Carl . . . and I've no idea what possibly could have moved him to provide such a gift. I don't remember ever voicing a complaint . . .

In any case, any cultist looking to elevate their craft should most definitely go on a quest to obtain a shaker from Elevated Craft. Adam Craft, you are a genius, and your shaker design is superb. It closes! It opens! It keeps stuff inside even under the most vigorous and unnecessary level of agitation! Also, the in-built measuring cap with Imperial and Metric demarcations is incredibly handy. My wife's much put-upon ceramic measuring cups thank you. I'm amazed I didn't break any of them. Get this shaker. It makes every single recipe requiring a shaker infinitely easier. It also cleans up in two shakes of a pointy tail.

Virtually all of the glassware pictured in this tome is from my (possibly pathological) collection of barware. A *few* were embellished or invented, but most abide in a hostile occupation of the kitchen cabinets along the north wall of the Sanctum Savorum. Each was carefully selected. I am of the opinion that the glass is part of the recipe, and its sacred geometry and materials are an inherent part of the experience of the beverage. If you can, select something close to what you see pictured to get the full effect. Certainly you should not eschew a cocktail herein because you lack the precise conveyance I've recommended . . . just don't send us pictures of Solo cups, please. Some things cannot be unseen.

A WORD OF CAUTION

Naturally, you are expected to imbibe responsibly. Many of these concoctions are quite potent. Go not by taste alone, for strength may be hidden in honeyed brews and salubrious solutions. Just as you would definitely say all the words, so too should you observe all the proper cautions related to the types of indulgences you shall find in these pages. You have been warned.

Aberrations and Variations upon Classic Libations

a. remains of style
b. pedicel

CTHULHU TAKES MANHATTAN

Manhattan like you've never tasted it! This time, it's not the city that isn't sleeping . . .

SACRIFICES

1 Key lime
2 ounces Four Roses bourbon
1 ounce dry vermouth
1 ounce Dad's Blue cream soda
1 ounce Daily's sweet and sour mix

THE RITUAL

Carve roughly three spirals from the skin of the lime, taking care to leave them attached to the lime. Carve ye now an X in the bottom of the fruit and crush the life from it into the waiting chalice. Add each of the other liquid offerings, stir, and place the lime, with spiral spread, in the glass.

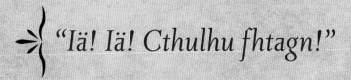 *"Iä! Iä! Cthulhu fhtagn!"*

SUNKEN ISLAND ICED TEA

Swim in the currents of flowing of spirits and companion nectars that lurk below the beckoning foam atop. Drink deep!

ARTIFACTS

1 Key lime
½ ounce triple sec
½ ounce white rum
½ ounce 1800 Coconut tequila
½ ounce gin
½ ounce vodka
Splash of cranberry-grape juice
¼ ounce agave nectar
Coconut-flavored seltzer

DISCOVERY

Squeeze half of the Key lime into the tall vessel; you will place the other half into the bottom of the glass. Pour in the spirits and mix well. Let the red-purple juice splash into the agave nectar and mix. Sink all down below a heavy layer of ice. Top with the effervescent and serve with a bamboo straw.

> "That is not dead which can eternal lie, and with strange eons even death may die."
> —H. P. Lovecraft, *The Call of Cthulhu*

THE FINAL SYLLABLE

These flowers of evil are rooted in a garden of spicy ginger. Just make sure you say the words before sampling, not after.

AS IT IS WRITTEN

3 ounces Hendrick's gin

2 ounces St-Germain elderflower liqueur

2 ounces ginger beer

2 ounces maraschino cherry juice

1 ounce fresh lime juice

1 ounce Hpnotiq liqueur

2 maraschino cherries

THE INVOCATION

When knoweth thee the damned words, retrieve the Cylinder That Shakes from its cradle. Jumble the listed, except the cherries, but nerves of ice thou must have to withstand the strain! Into the goblet then pour all, garnished with the Crimson Orbs of Mara'schin-o!

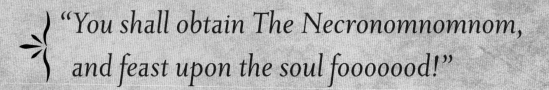

"You shall obtain The Necronomnomnom, and feast upon the soul fooooood!"

THE ANCIENT WAY

Pure, premium antiquity, this is a classy drink for contemplation and storytelling to the sound of waves or a crackling fire.

PRECEDENTS

1 raw sugar cube
2 dashes Angostura bitters
3 ounces Aberlour Speyside Single Malt Scotch
3 dashes spring water

THE BLESSING

Douse the six-faceted dulcet crystal in the bitter sap and grind in a hallowed bowl until viscous. Pour the ancient spirit into an ice-strewn glass fashioned by the Old Ones. Fill the spirit with the offering from the bowl and sprinkle the water of spring upon this as they mingle. Stir gently and sip from the cup as our forefathers and mothers did in epochs past!

"And sometimes at night the deep waters of the sea have grown clear and phosphorescent, to grant me glimpses of the ways beneath. And these glimpses have been as often of the ways that were and the ways that might be . . ."
—H. P. Lovecraft, "The White Ship"

MOSCOW GHOUL

The mule may be a common beast on bar tops these days, but the ghoul has access to so many more subtly buried flavors. Beneath the sweet surface / lie hints of flowers once lain above / Fragrances and intimations among the . . . bolder . . . flavors.

THE REMAINS

4 ounces ginger beer
2 ounces vodka
½ ounce lime juice
½ ounce St-Germain elderflower liqueur
Lindt Excellence Orange Intense dark chocolate, grated, for garnish

EXHUMATION

In an earthenware vessel, bury the remains, except for the chocolate, under crushed ice. Disturb roughly, wet the rim of the cup, and cast the grave dirt over the surfaces generously.

"Someone has placed flowers on this grave recently."
"No, look, they grow from below!"
"But, there was nothing there, yesterday . . . !"

THE DOOM THAT CAME TO SAZERAC

An invigoratingly twisted take, this complex potion is one to enjoy at a leisurely pace—for who knows what tomorrow brings?

WHAT WAS TAKEN

Ice 101 peppermint schnapps to wash glass

4 whiskey stones

2½ ounces brandy

3 dashes Peychaud's bitters

2 dashes Angostura bitters

1 sugar cube

½ teaspoon cold water

Lime peel for garnish

WHAT IS CAST DOWN

Rinse a glass of chilled rocks in the icy spirit of those cast into the lake. Throw the stones of their city on top of them, and set aside.

In a hand cauldron, mix the bitter and sweet with the water. Stir with ice until chilled, then strain into the prepared glass. Twist the green tendril in detestation of Bokrug, and cast this too into the glass.

> "And because they did not like the gray sculptured monoliths of Ib they cast these also into the lake . . ."
>
> —H. P. Lovecraft, "The Doom That Came to Sarnath"

MOJITOTEP

This husky elixir will have your "wrapped" attention after the first sip. A yummy mummy indeed.

LINIMENTS

3 mint leaves, plus I mint sprig for garnish
I teaspoon sugar
Pinch of mummy dust (or cinnamon if unavailable)
2 ounces white rum of the Bacardian bat
3 ice cubes, crushed
Club soda

MUMMIFICATION

With the moon in Saturn, invoke the spell of the forsaken Pharaoh. In a rocks glass, muddle the mint leaves with the sugar and mummy dust. Add the rum and crushed ice. Stir well and complete with club soda. Garnish with a mint sprig. Consume, or commune, via straw.

"In 1912, Emilio [Bacardi] and his wife travelled to Egypt, where he purchased a mummy . . ."
—Wikipedia

THE COSMICPOLITAN

Fancy a cosmic cosmo coalescing characterfully? This is for you. Not far off familiar shores but ready to see you into new gulfs.

THE WHITE SPACE

2 ounces chilled vodka

2 ounces Cointreau orange liqueur

I ounce unsweetened white grapefruit juice

Juice of I Key lime (about I ounce)

Dash of Chambord raspberry liqueur

THE COLD ABYSS

Let all reel together unheeding in an ice-filled shaker. Strain into a rime-frosted martini glass. Stalk on—where no spirit dares rove—and dwell in bliss on the far Arctic isle.

Past the wan-moon'd abysses of night,
I have liv'd o'er my lives without number,
I have sounded all things with my sight

—H. P. Lovecraft, "Nemesis"

ALHAZRED WHAT SHE'S HAVING

Sally forth to ecstasy as these favorite four play seductively for your pleasure. Don't be surprised if your ecstasy draws attention. IÄ! IÄ! IÄ! IÄ!

RAVINGS

1 ounce arabica coffee
1 ounce coffee liqueur
1 ounce amaretto
1 ounce Irish cream liqueur

IT'S COMING!

Into a sipping pipe, pour the black ichors of Kafé, follow with the nutty amber. The cream comes last. Revel in orgiastic glee, for mankind's climax nears!

"We drift on a chartless, resistless sea. Let us sing when we can, and forget the rest."
—H. P. Lovecraft, *Selected Letters*

BLOODY DERBY

More spirited than the original, old Ephraim would be proud. All fire and potence, this one is!

THE THINGS IN THE SHAKER

Lemon juice, for the rim

Rosemary salt, for the rim

4 ounces tomato juice

2 ounces vodka

1 ounce dry vermouth

1 ounce gin

½ ounce lime juice

¼ ounce balsamic vinegar

Dash of Worcestershire sauce

6 drops sriracha

2 cherry tomatoes for garnish

Lime wedge for garnish

THE MADHOUSE

This ancient marinara needs a rime of lemon juice and rosemary salt. Fill the glass with ice and let it sit.

In the . . . vessel, combine the remaining (save the sriracha, tomatoes, and lime wedge)—the strongest will win out, but not for long. Give it six drops of the heat from far places. They'll all be mightily shaken at the end, so much strain! Right in the cup they go. Garnish with the tomatoes and lime wedge. Serve promptly. Don't . . . . Waite.

"The flame—the flame . . .
beyond body, beyond life . . . ."
—H. P. Lovecraft, "The Thing on the Doorstep"

THE GLOOM THAT CAME TO SARNATH

Stormy and dark, this gorgeous concoction is almost too beautiful to desecrate by imbibng—but you know you must . . .

THE WEALTH OF SARNATH

2 large basil leaves
1 ounce Hendrick's gin
½ ounce simple syrup
Champagne or sparkling wine
6 blackberries for garnish

FROM OUT OF THE DEPTHS

To shreds they were cut, those soft green things! Thrown in to be berried, mangled, and muddled under the spirit, under the syrup! And a single frozen block on top to shake them with. This was poured without strain over the ice, and with bubbled wine did they celebrate, pouring it blasphemously on top of those they had vanquished. One of their heads and soft green bodies on a skewer did they leave, to show the Kingdoms of Kadatheron, Thraa, and Ilarnek what they had done to the Beings of Ib.

"Each year there was celebrated in Sarnath the feast of the destroying of Ib, at which time wine, song, dancing, and merriment of every kind abounded."

—H. P. Lovecraft, "The Doom That Came to Sarnath"

THE THIRD OATH

The waves beckon. The moonlight glitters. Strength lies beneath the surface . . . and soon within. The initiated yearn for the swirling darkness below—and to be carried into the embrace of power!

SACRAMENTS

3 ounces pomegranate juice

1 ounce vodka

1 ounce Pama pomegranate liqueur

1 ounce blue curaçao

1 ounce Pucker grape schnapps

1 ounce peach schnapps

1 ounce 1800 Coconut tequila

THE CONGRESS

There is no need to be gentle, these waves should break over the jagged icy shore in their revels and be conjoined in Dagon's tall and comely vessel . . .

"I would never die, but would live with those who had lived since before man ever walked the earth."

—H. P. Lovecraft, *The Shadow Over Innsmouth*

TSATHOGGUA'S SUNSET

Assuage your thirst with a refreshing take on a classic. New blood is always welcome, right?

SINKING SIGHTS

4 ounces orange juice
2 ounces tequila
½ ounce Pama pomegranate liqueur
½ ounce grenadine
Slab of watermelon

INTO DARKNESS

Chill darkness must take the bright juice and golden spirit, rattling them over the ice before straining into a tall flute (you can hear the flutes, can't you?). Invert a small ladle over the thus poured and add the blood-colored Ones slowly. Let them sink. Fit the pyramidal slab over them to hold below what should remain buried.

"Ebion saw that Zhothaqquah was indeed a god of his word: for the scene beyond the panel was nothing that could ever find a legitimate place in the topography of Mhu Thulan or of any terrestrial region."

—Clark Ashton Smith, *The Door to Saturn*

HAUNTER OF THE DARK-ARITA

In a dark place? Yearning for new vistas or insights beyond the ken of mortals? Inspiration comes from strange places—and not without price. Do you dare plumb the depths of this sweet darkness?

IN THE DARKNESS

4 ounces tequila
2 ounces grape schnapps
½ ounce fresh lime juice, plus more for the rim
1 ounce blackberry lemonade
Dash of sweet and sour mix
Black salt, for rim

THE TRI-LOBED EYE OPENS!

Make the Spiraling Sign over the shaking ice, and serve—in a vessel appropriate, rimmed with the juice of lime and black volcanic salt.

"Yog-Sothoth save me—
the three-lobed burning eye . . ."
—H. P. Lovecraft, "The Haunter of the Dark"

PALLID CARCOSA

A mellow, yellow classic with a double moon's shine over its frozen waves.
A delight fit for a King—and that's the Truth!

INHABITANTS

5 ounces pineapple juice
3 ounces coconut cream
2 ounces spiced rum
2 ounces peach moonshine
1 ounce sweet and sour mix
Cherries for rim

DRINK IN YELLOW

In a blender with ice all mix.
To edge of glass cherries afix.

Along the shore the cloud waves break,
The twin suns sink behind the lake

—Robert W. Chambers, *The King in Yellow*

DREAMLANDER SLAMMER

Fizzing with succulent energies, this dream-in-a-glass is one that will stick with you. Subtle colors and bold flavors combine for a result you won't sour on, and they may haunt you.

INGREDIENTS

5 ounces orange juice

2 ounces triple sec

2 ounces Pucker grape schnapps

1½ ounces amaretto

1 ounce Hendrick's gin

AWAKEN TO DREAMS

Combine all in a shaker full of ice, shake—shake until the subject rouses! Splash this cold draught into a large glass filled with ice. Sip and remember. Sip and forget.

> "Wise men have interpreted dreams, and the gods have laughed."
> —H. P. Lovecraft, "Hypnos"

BLUEBERRY DEVILRY

This daiquiri is devilishly seductive, with a blend of both tropical and higher-latitude spirits and flavors. Sink into the darkness, and show your horns.

HELLRAISERS

1 cup blueberries
1 cup crushed ice
3 ounces rum
2 ounces brandy
1 ounce coconut rum
¼ ounce agave syrup
½ ounce sweet and sour mix
½ ounce lime juice
Watermelon "horns" to garnish

THROW THE HORNS

Under a descending crescent moon, blend all thy wild spirits and familiars smooth. Serve in a wide, low cauldron with the horns a-showing! Cackle madly.

"The Devil pulls the strings which make us dance . . ."
—Charles Baudelaire

THE GREAT OLD ONES

Four of the oldest combine in a powerful double measure of potence. Dare you open these four vessels, only to slam them moments later?

THE FOUR WHO MUST BE NAMED

¾ ounce Glenmorangie Single Malt Scotch

¾ ounce Four Roses bourbon

¾ ounce Gordon's London Dry gin

¾ ounce Bushmills Irish whiskey

ALL SHALL BE CONSUMED

Let them come forth from their prisons into the slender vessel of twice height, ¾ each, that the crystal prison shall be full! Let their power course into thee, and let the warmth and madness spread in the new host! Iä! Iä the Four Who Are One!

"The Old Ones were, the Old Ones are, and the Old Ones shall be. Not in the spaces we know, but between them, They walk serene and primal, undimensioned and to us unseen."
—H. P. Lovecraft, "The Dunwich Horror"

HELL RESIDENTE

Even the damned and their wardens need something to look forward to at the end of a long and timeless day of torment. Can't have the residents becoming inured, and you don't want the demons getting bored. The Hell Residente is just the right damned thing to take the edge off, whether you are sharpening your anticipation of tomorrow's tortures or the tines of your pitchfork.

SIN-GREDIENTS

1½ ounces white rum
¾ ounce blue curaçao
¾ ounce dry vermouth
½ ounce Fireball cinnamon whiskey
½ ounce Hell-Cat Maggie Irish whiskey
½ ounce grenadine
1 slice blood orange

THE PATH OF DAMNATION

Fill a shaker with ice—for Hell hath frozen over. Combine the litany of sin-gredients, except for the orange, and shake as you contemplate your fate. Pour into a martini glass and add a slice of blood orange to garnish your wages of sin.

But when thou art again in the sweet world,
I pray thee to the mind of others bring me;
No more I tell thee, and no more I answer.
—Dante Alighieri, *The Inferno*, Canto VI. 90

SCALEY NAVAL

Scurvy be th' least o' your worries with this draught in hand! Banish yer thirst t' the deeps with tropical tides and sun-flecked cinnamon. If you listen close, ye can hear . . . well, 'tis best not said aloud near the shallows . . .

RISING FROM THE DEEPS

2 ounces unsweetened pure white grapefruit juice

2 ounces peach moonshine

1 ounce Goldschläger cinnamon schnapps

GAZING INTO THE DEPTHS

All the contents o' that bathysphere will come out severely shaken. Put 'em on ice in a snifter, you'll need a deep one.

"Perhaps I should not hope to convey in mere words the unutterable hideousness that can dwell in absolute silence and barren immensity."
—H. P. Lovecraft, "Dagon"

MINT JU-LENG

A classicist's dream, this will fortify you for your journey into lands real and dreamt. Just keep clear which is which.

INGREDIENTS

3 mint leaves, plus 1 for garnish
1 teaspoon sugar
½ teaspoon rose water
3 ice cubes, crushed

¾ ounce Scotch
1 ounce bourbon
Splash of club soda

PREPARATION

In a rocks glass, muddle three mint leaves with sugar and rose water. Add the crushed ice. Pour the Scotch and bourbon over the ice. Add a splash of club soda and stir gently. Garnish with a mint leaf.

"As you know, the word *julep* comes from the Arabic *gulláb*, which in turn comes from the Persian *gol āb*, meaning 'rose water.'"

—From the cocktails notebook of the High Priest Not to Be Described. Translated by fearless explorer Marco Polo in 1280, during his travels across Outer Mongolia.

MIND REPLACER

This shot of the dark will take your mind off the everyday. Creamy-sweet java with a subtle kick and smooth finish. See where it takes you . . .

PREPARE FOR TRANSFERENCE

2 ounces coffee liqueur
2 ounces vodka
2 ounces cream soda

ASSUME THE VESSEL

Let seep slowly the darkest memory first, trickling down the walls of thought. Then, the same do with the crystal clarity of mind, and lastly and again, the sweet effervescence of completion. The vessel is full; empty it into yourself and let surge the spirits you shall carry within.

"Later, as the earth's span closed, the transferred minds would again migrate through time and space . . ."
—H. P. Lovecraft, *The Shadow Out of Time*

DEMURELY CLOTHED LADY

Under those fine layers, a svelte and seductive flavor emerges, teasing you with dark hints of forbidden fruits. Will you set your lips to the edge of her glass and peer beneath the veil?

THE RAIMENT

1½ ounces Bacardí Black dark rum

1½ ounces dry vermouth

⅓ ounce brandy

⅓ ounce grenadine

⅓ ounce peach schnapps

⅓ ounce fresh lemon juice

1 blackberry for garnish

THE ENSEMBLE

Give it all a little shake, but not too much—that wouldn't be decorous. Pour into a tall cool glass. Adorn with the blackberry. Turn heads.

"Almost nobody dances sober, unless they happen to be insane."
—H. P. Lovecraft

PINK FLAMI-GO

A refreshing and unexpected journey. This experience will leave you flying high and feeling free of your usual routine. You'll find chemistry with this one!

INSIDE THE METAL CYLINDER

Dried butterfly pea flower blossoms

1½ ounces white rum

1 cup lemonade

½ cup lemon-lime soda

1 ounce crème de menthe liqueur

.02 cc LorAnn's cinnamon oil

Ice

ALCHEMICAL PROCESS

Place the blossoms in the rum for one full planetary rotation. The infusion will take on a deep indigo hue. The blossoms can be removed with little strain.

The primary metallic vessel should be used to combine all the other reagents. Insert the tip of a wooden probe into the oil. Stir briefly, and then discard the probe. Begin a thirty second agitation procedure. The contents should then be poured over ice, with the violet catalyst served in tandem. When the subject is ready, it may pour the catalyst over its beverage to witness the reaction.

"They were pinkish things about five feet long; with crustaceous bodies bearing vast pairs of dorsal fins or membraneous wings and several sets of articulated limbs, and with a sort of convoluted ellipsoid, covered with multitudes of very short antennae, where a head would ordinarily be."

—H. P. Lovecraft, "The Whisperer in Darkness"

BLOOD BATH & BEYOND

The blood is the life, but the drink is the life of the party. Darksome desires and subtle pleasures seethe below the viscous surface, awaiting the descent of your lips to bring the ecstasy that consumes. . . . Drink deep.

VITAE

2 ounces Carnivor cabernet sauvignon

2 ounces Chambord raspberry liqueur

2 ounces cranberry-grape juice

½ ounce blue curaçao

THE KILL

Swirl the contents appreciatively in a wide wine goblet, admiring the ruby colors and silky texture.

"There was a deliberate voluptuousness which was both thrilling and repulsive, and as she arched her neck she actually licked her lips like an animal, till I could see in the moonlight the moisture shining on the scarlet lips and on the red tongue as it lapped the white sharp teeth. Lower and lower went her head . . . I closed my eyes in a languorous ecstasy and waited—waited with a beating heart."

—Bram Stoker, *Dracula*

WHISKEY FEZ

Refresh your spirit (or, some spirit . . .) with this beauty. It serves as well as you do, so why not reward all your eldritch labors with this sweet and zesty respite?

WHAT IS OFFERED

3 raspberries, plus 1 raspberry sprig for garnish
1 ounce fresh lemon juice
2 ounces blended Scotch
Pinch of superfine brown sugar
4 ounces cream soda

COMPLETE THE RITE

The number of the raspberries shall be three, and first into the steel they go, followed by ice, the bitter juice fresh of the lemon, and the spirit. With vigor toss them until icy frost creeps into your hand. Into a tall glass put the fine sugar, and then pour in what emerges from the steel cup. Top with the soda, and be satisfied.

"To be bitter is to attribute intent and personality to the formless, infinite, unchanging and unchangeable void."
—H. P. Lovecraft

INNSMOUTH DEPTH CHARGE

Smoke on the firewater! This unholy trinity has some . . . depth . . . to it, and you'll get a charge out of it!

MUNITIONS

1 ounce Gilbey's gin
1 ounce Admiral Nelson's coconut rum
10 ounces Jack's Abby Smoke & Dagger black lager

THE ASSAULT

Carefully combine the incendiaries in a shot glass, then drop the charge into the beer—and give 'em Hell!

"Y'ha-nthlei was not destroyed when the upper-earth men shot death into the sea. It was hurt, but not destroyed."

—H. P. Lovecraft, *The Shadow Over Innsmouth*

NEGRONI-NOMICON

Savory, with a hint of the sinfully exotic. Delve into southern latitudes strewn with forbidden ruins and dark flavors. "Campari! Vermouth! Negroni!"

DREAD CONTENTS

1 ounce gin
1 ounce Campari liqueur
1 ounce dry vermouth
1 ounce triple sec
1 ounce blue curaçao

WHAT IS SUMMONED

Build ye this fell elixir over the icy wastes of glass of the old fashion. When all the spirits are present, stir them until an even and unnatural blue radiance suffuses the icy depths. Then you will know you have succeeded.

> "The ice desert of the South and the sunken isles of Ocean hold stones whereon Their seal is engraven, but who hath seen the deep frozen city or the sealed tower . . . ?"
>
> —H. P. Lovecraft, "The Dunwich Horror"

THE ESOTERIC WATER OF DAGON

When one drinks of the abyss, the abyss also consumes thee. . . . Submerge yourself in the frothing darkness and taste the colors.

THE RITE STUFF

1 ounce Pepsi
½ ounce vodka
1 ounce Baileys Irish cream liqueur
1 ounce blue curaçao
½ ounce amaretto

TAKING THE OATH

Aside shall you hold the Ko-la in the final chalice. Impregnate the shaking vessel with the four spirits vigorously. The skin of the vessel should grow cold when the deed is done. Rest briefly; and then, straining mightily pour ungently the admixture into the chalice. Iä Dagon! Iä, Iä Cthulhu fhtagn!

"The natives did not like him to drink and talk with strangers; and it was not always safe to be seen questioning him."

—H. P. Lovecraft, *The Shadow Over Innsmouth*

THE STRANGE HIGHBALL IN THE MIST

A classic taken to new heights! Dramatic and mysterious, and yet familiar. . . . Mind that first step.

FOR THE JOURNEY

4 or 5 ice cubes

1½ ounces Scotch

1 ounce Coca Cola

5 ounces club soda

3 small bars dry ice

Water

WHAT IS LEARNED

Place a glass of tall apex in a level-bottomed basin. Place the frozen blocks of ice in the glass, and within pour the Highland spirit and the dark ichor. Add then the frothing liquid. Stir well. Arrange the strange ices in the basin, around the glass, and slowly let pour in enough water to summon the mists. Serve with haste.

> "In the morning mist comes up from the sea by the cliffs beyond Kingsport. White and feathery it comes from the deep to its brothers the clouds, full of dreams of dank pastures and caves of leviathan."
> —H. P. Lovecraft, "The Strange High House in the Mist"

UNCHARTED WATERS

GROG-SOTHOTH

Above decks or below, this'll keep you warm as you tack into the evening breeze, or make merry with your mates down below. Let it be the key to your next pleasure cruise.

KEY WORTHIES

1 teaspoon dark brown sugar
8 ounces hot water
Pinch of powdered cinnamon
Juice of 1 Key lime (about 1 ounce)
2 ounces Stonekeep Meadery Hibiscus Metheglyn mead
4 ounces Calico Jack spiced rum
1 cinnamon stick for garnish

TREAD THE WAVES

Dissolve ye the brown sugar in the vapor-giving waters. Stir in the spice exotic. Add ye now the lime juice, mead, and rum. Serve in a worthy vessel, with a rod of cinnamon, and keep the scurvy—and sanity—away!

"If ye be brave or fool enough to face a pirate's curse, proceed."
—Davy Jones, *Pirates of the Caribbean: Dead Man's Chest*

THE ROOTBEER
OF ALL EVIL

Smooth and sultry, this towering glass of chill darkness is sinfully delicious. Just don't let the clergy see you with one (they'll be jealous).

THE SINS OF THE FATHERS

9 ounces Dad's Old Fashioned root beer
3 ounces ginger beer
¾ ounce Scotch
¾ ounce bourbon
¾ ounce gin
¾ ounce Irish whiskey

AB-SOLUTION

In a tall and frosted glass possessed of few and icy virtues, combine all the sins and blend them with a turning and stirring. The sin-drinker be praised, for they washeth away our guilt!

"One man's theology is another man's belly laugh."
—Robert A. Heinlein

THE KING IN JELL-O

Pallid snacks with a surprise ending. No reason for stage fright with a little rehearsal.

THE REVELERS

2 envelopes Knox plain gelatin
¼ cup cold water
½ cup white sugar, divided
½ cup fresh lemon juice
6 ounces limoncello

THE PLAY'S THE THING

In middle-sized craft of potter, sprinkle gelatin over cold water.

Allow to bloom for minutes ten, or until can be seen no dry gelatin.

Into the chamber of waves so small, for thirty seconds or until melted all.

Add slowly half the sweet white grains, and mix and stir till none remains.

Let temperature fall to that of room, then in this mix the juice and spirit entomb.

Pour well mix'd into your mold, and for six hours let stay cold.

The remaining sugar in bowl equipping, to provide to guests for dipping.

"If to be fair is to be beautiful," he said, "who can compare with me in my white mask?"
—Robert W. Chambers, *The King in Yellow*

RUM BEYOND

What delicacies and exotic invisibilities swirl around us, unknown and untasted? Can such strange things coexist harmoniously? Do you dare open all your eyes, and your lips, to discovery?

COMPONENTS

4 ounces aloe vera drink with pulp (the big chunky kind)
Juice and pulp of ¼ lime
3 ounces silver coconut rum
Lime peel or aloe vera leaf for garnish

THE EXPERIMENT

Pour the aloe base directly into a glass; crush the quartered lime and scrape the pulp in as well. Shake the rum over the ice for thirty seconds and strain into the glass. Stir vigorously to get everything swirling.

Express the curled lime skin or aloe vera stem gently and garnish at points around the rim of the glass, dipping into the results of your experiment.

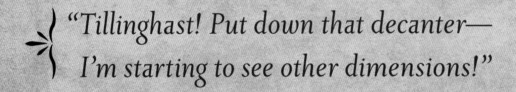

*"Tillinghast! Put down that decanter—
I'm starting to see other dimensions!"*

HP-NOTIQ REGRESSION

This psychotropical citrus floral mélange won't be easily forgotten. Mesmerizing cerulean depths rise and beckon you to a new taste experience, or . . . is it? Sweet memories come in waves to lap at the edge of the glass and call to something deeply submerged in you.

BELOW THE SURFACE

Large round ice cube

2 ounces Reyka vodka

I ounce 1800 Coconut tequila

½ ounce St-Germain elderflower liqueur

I ounce Hpnotiq liqueur

½ ounce blue curaçao

5 drops pure cranberry juice

MEMORY STIRS

See the shape in your mind, pore over it carefully, in the order remembered. See! See the crimson splash from the straw—center, and all four directions! Remember, the dripping red!

"Ocean is more ancient than the mountains, and freighted with the memories and dreams of Time."

—H. P. Lovecraft, "The White Ship"

COOL PEAR

This exotic potion will definitely help keep you from overheating. A hint of the cold void behind the world we know, and then sweeter tones seize and sharpen your perception. Just what the doctor ordered!

INGREDIENTS

5 ounces Asian pear saké
4 ounces aloe vera drink with pulp
½ ounce Ice 101 Blue Arctic Mint peppermint schnapps

PREPARATION

In a shaker full of ice (so frozen!), mix all the ingredients. Pour into a chilled (so chill!) tulip glass with ice (so icy!).

> Heed the learned Doctor, for overindulgence may lead to severe . . . "impearment."

The end is here.
No more ice – the man looked
and ran away. Warmer every minute, and the
I fancy you know what
tissues can't last.
the nerves and the
I said about the will and the
organs ceased to work.
keep up indefinitely
preserved body after
I had not foreseen
It was good
killed him. the
There was
so – he had to
place where we had
Dr. Torres
and they
couldn't s
I had
get me
work again.
artificial preservation
my letter and
that time
organs never
tried
years ago
for you

THE SHADOW OUT OF LIME

This jolt of citrus might make you lose time, though you certainly won't waste it.

THOSE WHO WILL TRAVEL

2 ounces lime vodka
2 ounces lime tequila
½ ounce lime juice
Splash of extra dark rum
Black volcanic salt

THE JOURNEY FORWARD

Two spirits shall inhabit the same salt-rimed vessel. To them add the fresh juice of the lime. Plunge the shadowy ichor into these from on high. Begin the transference.

"Primal myth and modern delusion joined in their assumption that mankind is only one—perhaps the least—of the highly evolved and dominant races of this planet's long and largely unknown career."

—H. P. Lovecraft, *The Shadow Out of Time*

THE MOON-GROG

It's not a hallucination, this rum-based tropical vision isn't for spectators.
Join the revels!

FANCIES

4 ounces piña colada mix
1½ ounces Malibu rum
1½ ounces lemon-lime soda
1 ounce white rum
¼ cup crushed ice
Blue edible glitter

THE VISION MADE REAL

To the sound of otherworldly flutes, shake all the ingredients with ice. Strain to those sinister strains and serve cold.

"Terrible and piercing was the shaft of ruddy refulgence that streamed through the Gothic window, and the whole chamber was brilliant with a splendour intense and unearthly."

—H. P. Lovecraft, "The Moon-Bog"

THE SILVER WHIS-KEY

Glinting like fragments of a half-remembered dream, a perfect dram to reflect upon vistas lit by otherworldly night. There for you when the need is argent.

DREAM TO AWAKEN

Chrome whiskey stones
2 ounces silver tequila
2 ounces silver rum
2 ounces moonshine

AWAKEN TO DRAM

Fill your cup with silvery cubes, long-chilled in the frigid air. Upon these pour out the argent liquids, and stirring (but not awakening), sip the water of dreams.

"At night, when the objective world has slunk back into its cavern and left dreamers to their own, there come inspirations and capabilities impossible at any less magical and quiet hour."
—H. P. Lovecraft

OLD TITUS

That's no mule. . . . Cherry and ginger in balance, strengthened with whiskey plus funeral home florals. It'll change you.

THE BOURBON IS BENEATH

1¼ ounces Old Crow bourbon
¾ ounce St–Germain elderflower liqueur
4 ounces ginger beer
½ ounce fresh lemon juice
8 dashes Angostura bitters
½ ounce grenadine

TRANSITION

Into a tall, ice-filled glass, pour the bourbon. To this add the Saint's elixir and then the gingered brew (gingerly). Combine the others in a mixing glass and pour slowly into the main vessel. Let what lies beneath stir gently.

> "I am not very proud of being a human being; in fact, I distinctly dislike the species in many ways. I can readily conceive of beings vastly superior in every respect."
>
> —H. P. Lovecraft

THE WHITE SIP

Every voyage has the potential to land us on new shores. Over this sweet horizon, set sail for heavens undreamed of, where the only rocks are round and smooth—swirling in a private ocean of delights. Mind you don't sail over the edge in your bliss.

CREW

2 ounces vodka
2 ounces half-and-half
1½ ounces butterscotch schnapps
1½ ounces salted caramel liqueur
Large (preferably round) ice shape
Two triangles of white chocolate

THE VOYAGE

O'er the orb poured all those aboard
Stirred like sea foam and fog
A scalding blade cut the ivory sails
And becalmed, was received The White Sip.

"And I viewed by moonlight the sparkling sea, the crystal headlands, and the placid harbor wherein lay anchored the White Ship."
—H. P. Lovecraft, "The White Ship"

NIGHTGAUNT

Dream dark and take flight with this ticklesome fortified tea. It'll drop you in a happy place.

FROM THE DREAMLANDS

6 cups water, divided	2 family-sized black tea bags	1½ cups Irish whiskey
2 cups sugar	1 cinnamon stick	Ice
1 family-sized cinnamon orange tea bag	Black food coloring	Edible star sprinkles
	Edible silver glitter	1 sprig of fresh mint

TO BE BORNE ON LEATHERY WINGS

Bring ye first 4 cups of the water to boil. Add ye in the sugar, stir to dissolve, and thence all the tea and rod of sin-amon. In the cold wastes allow this to sit a full day.

Leave half the result in the cold, and to the rest add the black ichor and argent shards. This is then poured into the tray of multitudinous cubes and left to freeze solid.

Now, into a pitcher, the remaining syrupteascious fluid, final 2 cups of water, and the spirit as well. Cleanse this preparation of the bags and remove the rod.

Take the cubes of night and crush them with pulses of whirling blades. Do the same with an equal amount of simple ice.

In a fulsome glass, layer halfway with clear ice. Pour in a half measure of the tea, adding ice to maintain the level if needful. In the remainder, bury in the black shards and cast down the stars upon and within them! At the peak, more of the elixir—and a sprig of mint. Nightfall comes to the glass as black wings stretch down.

> "And worst of all, they never spoke or laughed, and never smiled because they had no faces at all to smile with."
> —H. P. Lovecraft, "Dreamquest of the Unknown Kadath"

SPACE MEAD

All aboard! This flight will leave you flying high on sweet spices with fruity layovers that will take you into uncharted territories of flavor. Recline your seat and enjoy the ride.

CARRY-ON ITEMS

2 ounces Stonekeep Meadery Meglethin spiced mead
2 ounces tonic water
1 ounce Scotch
1 ounce peach schnapps
1 ounce cranberry juice

PREFLIGHT PREPARATIONS

Over non-Euclidian ice, ladle all with care that which is to journey with you. After minor turbulence on takeoff, all should be smooth. Prepare for . . . departure.

"Barkeep, I better settle up—my flight is leaving."
"Sir, there's not an airport in a hundred miles of here . . ."
"Oh—there's no air where I'm going, either."

ROSEMARY'S MELONCOLY BABY

You can see the magic that goes into the birthing of such a potion. Colors swirl and combine into the unexpected flavors. Is that a watermelon? You'll be suckling at this one slowly. Raise it properly.

THE UNBORN

½ ounce Pama pomegranate liqueur
I ounce Pucker grape schnapps
½ ounce peach schnapps
½ ounce 1800 Coconut tequila
½ ounce vodka
I ounce tequila
Dash of blue curaçao
I ounce orange juice
Dash of grenadine
½ ounce sweet and sour mix

THE PROGENY

Labor to pour the seething spirits slowly, in order, over a large ice globe in a capacious tumbler. Soothe.

> "What's in this drink?"
> —Rosemary Woodhouse, *Rosemary's Baby*

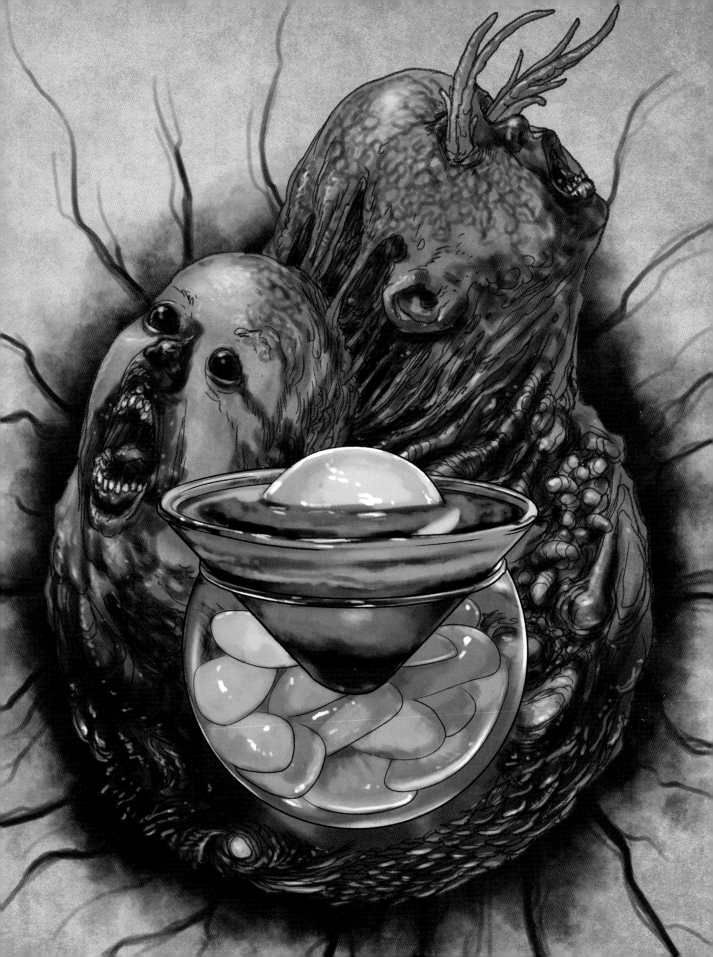

ABYSSAL DEPTHS

The familiar, sunny peaks of pineapple thrust up from azure depths over ancient stones alive with their own chill. The darkness suffuses the fruit as you allow yourself to sink into these depths, a final prize to savor as the tide recedes.

WHAT LURKS BELOW

Chilled whiskey stones
Pineapple slabs
2 ounces lemon-lime soda
3 ounces vodka
1 ounce blue curaçao

DEPTHS DO YOU TAKE PART

Stack the cyclopean blocks and atop them the xanthous slabs. In the order given, add the liquids, the last poured slowly over all.

"We live on a placid island of ignorance in the midst of black seas of infinity, and it was not meant that we should voyage far."
—H. P. Lovecraft, "The Call of Cthulhu"

KILL IT WITH FIRE!

Fighting eldritch horrors is thirsty work—and why should the monsters get all the flames? Spice things up with this high-octane flamethrower of a cocktail! You may want a chaser to pat the flames out.

INFLAMMABLES

Small piece of hot pepper
2 ounces tequila
½ ounce Scotch
½ ounce demerara syrup
¾ ounce lime juice
¼ ounce sweet vermouth
2 dashes Angostura bitters
2 dashes Peychaud's bitters

CONFLAGRATION

All right, this is how you prep your gear! First, mash the heat capsule real good in a tin. Put everything but the salt in a fuel mixer with some ice (don't ask—you aren't paid to think!) and shake it up with some muscle! Have a glass rimmed in that salt Col. Van Camp likes. Serve it up, boys! Serve it up!

> "What the thing was, he would never tell. It was like some of the carvings on the hellish altar, but it was alive."
> —H. P. Lovecraft, "The Case of Charles Dexter Ward"

MILK OF AMNESIA

Whatever you aim to forget, it won't be this utterly smooth flavor. Chocolate and black licorice crème go down so easy, you won't remember what was gnawing at you.

MEMORY FRAGMENTS

2 ounces black sambuca
1 ounce crème de cacao
1 ounce heavy cream

I THINK I JOGGED IT TOO HARD

Shake everything hard with ice and serve to the brutes of your squad.

"The most merciful thing in the world, I think, is the inability of the human mind to correlate all its contents."

—H. P. Lovecraft, "The Call of Cthulhu"

THE GROGGOTH

Let the wave of far C'trus crash upon the shores of your gums and dash themselves to oblivion against the rocky pegs of your teeth. You'll be shapeless in no time!

TO CREATE THE AMORPHOUS

One 3-ounce box lime Jell-O
1 cup boiling hot water
1 cup Midori melon liqueur
2 cups lemon-lime soda, divided
1 cup pineapple juice
1 cup plus 2 ounces blue curaçao, divided
1 teaspoon edible glitter

IT WILL SERVE!

One day before you begin, you must summon the gelid thing into your ritual bowl. One cup of water a'boil serves to dissolve it. When a day has passed, add the emerald spirit and one cup of the hybrid effervescence. Into the cold for hours three this shall go, until fully, horridly gelid.

From the bowl take what you have made and subject it to blades awhirl until near-liquid again. Add the juice, the cup of blue ichor, the remaining effervescent fluid, and the shining flakes. See it pulse gently.

Pour the Groggoth into a tall glass full of crushed ice, leaving generous space at the top.

Invert a concave utensil and pour the final measure of azure ichor atop it before serving.

> "It was the utter, objective embodiment of the fantastic novelist's 'thing that should not be.'"
>
> —H. P. Lovecraft, *At the Mountains of Madness*

RYE'LYEH RISING

It rises from the bottom—reaching for you with savory limbs! Complex and nuanced, sample flavors conjured from a banished, ancient deep, even as you are seduced by the alien beauty of what confronts you. To do otherwise would be . . . madness.

THE SLEEPERS

2 ounces dry vermouth
Splash of bitters
2 ounces rye
Drop of grenadine
Dried mango

THE AWAKENING

In a chalice clear, pour the dry vermouth and add the bitters. Pour the rye from a measuring cup against the edge of the glass slowly. It will lay atop the others. Carefully add the crimson drop to the center of the glass. Garnish with dried mango tendrils. Serve with devotion—and a cocktail straw.

"Ph'nglui mglw'nafh Cthulhu R'lyeh wgah'nagl fhtagn—"
—H. P. Lovecraft, "The Call of Cthulhu"

OLD R'LYEH

Take an island sunset, a swashbuckling trio of shady spirits, and waves broken by upthrusts of pure mystery—and press it all into a glass and then into your hand. You're in for some chop, and quite an adventure.

BENEATH THE WAVES

2 cups cut pineapple

2 cups demerara syrup

1 ounce Indian tonic water

1 ounce Key lime juice

1 ounce pineapple vinegar shrub

2 dashes Peychaud's bitters

½ ounce overproof rum

1 ounce white rum

1 ounce golden rum

1 ounce dark rum

THE SLEEPER AWAKENS

The rocks will tremble as all but the spirits are combined. Pour these over crushed ice, and then add ye the spirits light to dark, but the most powerful spirit shall be topmost should ye wish to summon flame.

TO DRAW FORTH THE SHRUB

Crush cubes of pineapple and add them and their juice to an equal amount of the sugar of Demerara. Chill this till morn, then strain into an equal part apple cider vinegar. Stir well. Bottle or use chilled. This part of the ritual yields enough for several visits to Old R'lyeh—should you wish to bring others on your journey.

> "Drinking is not a religion; it's hardly even a philosophy."
> —Bobby Derie, "The Old R'lyeh"

TEKILA-LI-LI

Whatever pace you choose, there's no escaping this chill specter. You can shoot it if you want, but it's still going to come at you like a subway train.

THE ECHOES

2 ounces silver tequila
½ ounce Gordon's London Dry gin
½ ounce Ice 101 peppermint schnapps
1 Gummy Blob (optional)
Ice (optional)

FROZEN IN HORROR!

Let the spirits mix into shapeless congeries, stir or shake them as much as you dare.

A double shot may dull the horror of what you have seen, but do not watch as the amorphous abomination crawls down the throats of your fellow explorers—and best to leave the formless mass out entirely when going that route.

If better taken in small sips, add to ice in a large glass, and look not too closely at the shape that lies in the depths!

"Unhappy act! Not Orpheus himself, or Lot's wife, paid much more dearly for a backward glance. And again came that shocking, wide-ranged piping—'Tekeli-li! Tekeli-li!'"

—H. P. Lovecraft, *At the Mountains of Madness*

BLASTED HEATH LANDSLIDE

A cosmically good dessert cocktail, swirling with an otherworldly combination of candy store favorites. You'll be consumed with the urge to have an Other.

IN THE WELL

2 ounces Godiva chocolate liqueur

2 ounces dark rum

2 ounces butterscotch schnapps

½ ounce Chambord raspberry liqueur

½ banana, quartered lengthwise

Heath candy crumbles

CONFECTION UNLEASHED

Place a few frozen stones or bits of ice in a low glass, onto which ye will strain the commingled liquids! Set the pallid tendrils upright, and sprinkle lightly with the changed bits of earthy gravel.

> "No other name could fit such a thing, or any other thing fit such a name."
> —H. P. Lovecraft, "The Colour Out of Space"

DE VERMIS MEZCALIS

Redolent of Mesoamerican spice and unexplored places, this potent concoction is not for the faint of still-beating heart. A gift from our crystal skull to yours, slip down jungled corridors to the thunder of hidden drums . . .

FORBIDDEN SPICES

Sal de Gusano to rim the glass

½ ounce agave nectar

1 ounce mezcal

1 ounce tequila

½ ounce Bombay Sapphire gin

½ ounce ginger ale, plus more for the rim

Dash of Angostura orange bitters

Drop of lime juice

THE WORM CONQUERS

Let flow the worm spice along the rim of the hollowed crystal skull. Dissolve the nectar in the measure of mezcal in a separate cup, then combine all in a shaker of ice. Pour with utmost care into the prepared skull.

"The Seven Gods of Chaos—slumber in their crystal prison, waiting to reclaim Earth . . . and burn the heavens."

—*De Vermis Mysteriis*, page 87, *Hellboy* (2004)

IN YOUR MOUTH WITH MADNESS

Sure to be a cult classic! Two tumblers up! A sweet and zesty romp chock-full of the right stars!

THE CAST

Coconut sugar to rim the glass
3 ounces 10 Cane rum
3 ounces brandy
½ ounce lime juice
2 ounces limeade

THE PLOT

"The story may get a little muddled—the elements are all thrown together and then right at ya—but it's got a sweet ending. Mug for the camera, and we'll get some good shots in. Be sure to rim that edge first, it's a lot harder once the cast is already chilling in the tub. The audience is gonna lap this up. Hey, do you drink sugar cane?"

"Where does madness leave off and reality begin?"
—H. P. Lovecraft, *The Shadow Over Innsmouth*

ABSIN-ATH WAITE

A complex spirit normally too powerful to combine plays well in strange company here. Dominant but well-attended, go for a wild ride with this vixen elixir and her outré friends.

GHOSTS IN THE SHELL

2 ounces absinthe
I ounce Pucker sour apple schnapps
3 chunks frozen pineapple
Fresh banana

GREEN-HUED BEAUTY

Two spirits shall vie for dominance as tensions build within the glass. Garnish artfully with the chunks of fruits mentioned in the Dole chants.

"I'll tell you something of the forbidden horrors she led me into. . . . Some people know things about the universe that nobody ought to know, and can do things that nobody ought to be able to do."

—H. P. Lovecraft, "The Thing on the Doorstep"

TCHO-TCHO-TCHOCOLATE

Delectable, creamy cocoa submerging powerful spirits and a spice that hints at dark secrets . . .

FOREIGN BODIES

2½ ounces Godiva chocolate liqueur
1½ ounces vodka
1 ounce saké
3 drops sriracha

SILKEN FIRE

Ancient secret: mix all together thoroughly, serve to the unsuspecting in a cordial glass for sipping. So smooth, but with a bite.

> "One who sits by the well will never go thirsty.
> One who falls in the well will be drunk."
>
> —Tcho-Tcho proverb

BEER
AND FEAR

H. PEACH LOVEDRAFT

The dark aura of this piece belies its light flavor. Don't judge this book by its cover, either—the surprise ending will sneak up on you. You won't be able to put it down till you're finished!

EXPOSITION

5 ounces draught Guinness Irish stout
2 ounces peach schnapps
1 ounce white rum

CLIMAX

Gently let flow the body of the work into a shaker of crushed ice. Edit lightly, and pour all, including the ice, into a large tumbler for the reader to digest.

"Atmosphere, not action, is the great desideratum of weird fiction."
—H. P. Lovecraft, "Notes on Writing Weird Fiction"

GUG-A-LUG

This fortified shandy was made to go down easy. Raise all your elbows and pour—it'll bring a smile to your maw.

RAW MATERIALS

8 ounces citrus wheat beer

6 ounces lemonade

2 ounces chilled vodka

TO BUILD

In a glass of cyclopean proportions, pour the beer, followed by the lemon drink and the icy spirit. Stir gently and serve.

> "Of course all our respected forbears indulged in the flowing bowl to such an extent as to make fishes seem land animals by comparison."
>
> —H. P. Lovecraft to Zealia Brown Reed, February 13, 1928, *The Spirit of Revision*

THE LURKING BEER

Muse upon lightning-blasted forestscapes and twisting darksome tunnels with this roasty, nutty, hideously fortified draught. And, seeing that madness is best shared with a friend, there's enough to take someone with you . . .

THE STORM

6 ounces Blue Moon Iced Coffee Blonde wheat ale
6 ounces Samuel Smith's Nut brown ale
2 ounces Monkey Shoulder Scotch

THE REVELATION

Combine all the elements of the storm with gentle shaking to mix. Pour into a chilled beer mug. Use the remains to make another, and serve in two places at once! Shudder. Shudder at the approach of the lightning, and think not of those hills!

"Some said the thunder called the lurking fear out of its habitation, while others said the thunder was its voice."

—H. P. Lovecraft, "The Lurking Fear"

PICKMAN'S MODELO

Everyone wants to look their best, and this handsome devil will help put you in the right frame of mind. The darkness conceals twisting corridors of flavor, right under your nose!

CORPUS DELECTABLE

Hot sauce to rim the glass

2 ounces reposado tequila

1 ounce fresh lime juice

Drop of habanero hot sauce

½ ounce agave nectar

12 ounces Modelo Negra beer

Spicy chili salt for the rim

Jalapeño or lime wheel for garnish

DISINTERMENT

Artfully rub the rim of a highball glass with the spicy sauce. Shade in tequila, fresh lime, pepper juice, and agave to a shaker. Shake these, for it pleases the palate better, and strain over fresh ice. Top off with the beer. Serve remaining Modelo Negra with the cocktail. Garnish the rim with spicy chili salt and jalapeño or lime wheel.

> "Richard Upton Pickman, the greatest artist I have ever known—and the foulest being that ever leaped the bounds of life into the pits of myth and madness."
>
> —H. P. Lovecraft, "Pickman's Model"

THE DIREWULF

Some nights you just have to seize by the throat. Let these three spirits rampage down yours in a rush, and you'll be howling at the moon and scenting the night air with new vigor in no time. Dark, smooth, and surprising—and best enjoyed decisively. Don't look, leap!

THE PACK

5 ounces Wolf King imperial stout
2 ounces chilled Nooku bourbon cream
I ounce frozen Paddy's Irish whiskey

THE HOWL AND THE WHY

Pour the spirit of the wolf over a large icy sphere. Separately, combine the other two spirits in a shaker of ice and strain these over the sphere. Imbibe rapidly, lest the dire spirits howls curdle the blood and froth upon the lips. Rip wide the maw and let course the Wulf!

"Would you offer your throat to the wolf with the red roses?"

—Meatloaf, "You Took the Words Right Out of My Mouth"

MISSISSIPPI BONER

A stand-up cocktail for those about to rock! It's a tall cool one that's still smokin' hot and won't have you singing the blues. Conjure up a memorable night.

FOREPLAY THAT FUNKY MUSIC

Drop of liquid smoke
4 ounces Crown Royal Canadian whisky
6 ounces Samuel Adams cream stout

ROCK HARD

You'll need a hefty pair of frozen spheres. Put those in a tall glass with a drop of smoke (mirrors optional). Add the hard stuff, and then pour a stiff measure until your stout has a good head.

> "This transformation's such a terrible thing my body aches and screams as the beast is unleashed."
> —Mississippi Bones, "Full Moon Risin"

BEER THE FERMENTATIONS OF THE LEMON

What is a lemon wheel compared to the spirit distilled from it? Let its strength suffuse you in this warrior's draught of honey and citrus-fortified beer. Do you want to live forever?

WHAT IS BEST IN LIFE

3 ounces limoncello
2 ounces traditional mead
12 ounces Belgian white beer

CRUSH YOUR THIRST

Long ago, warriors sank the spirits of C'trus and the nectar of the gods into their hazy cups of beer, and Crom laughed from his fountain.

"The more I see of what you call civilization, the more highly I think of what you call savagery!"
—Robert E. Howard

THE DEVIL'S HOPYARD

Thou cans't try to keep the Devil at arm's length, but sendeth He his Hell-Cats and Fireballs at ye! This cinnamon-tinged marathon draught will keep you hopping for a good while.

THE CABAL

2 ounces Hell-Cat Maggie Irish whiskey
1 ounce Fireball cinnamon whiskey
Victory HopDevil IPA

REVEL!

In the yard glass, spill the liquid form of the Devil's fire and familiar, and fill the rest with the HopDevil himself!

"In Heaven, there is no beer. That's why we drink it here!"
—Ernst Neubach

DIVINE
INVENTIONS

THE WINE-ING TRAPEZOHEDRON

Dark and alluring, this is a journey of taste where expectation serves you not. A perfect draught for sipping and the sharing of wisdom at length. Just stay out of the light . . .

INSIDE THE CONTAINER

5 ounces cabernet sauvignon
2 ounces Bacardi dark rum
½ ounce lime juice
2 dashes Peychaud's bitters
Tonic water

DARK VISTAS UNDREAMED

Pour all but the last into the metal cylinder of ice. Humming the Dhôl Chants, shake until icy cold. Strain into a faceted glass and top with tonic.

"It was treasured and placed in its curious box by the crinoid things of Antarctica, salvaged from their ruins by the serpent-men of Valusia, and peered at aeons later in Lemuria by the first human beings."
—H. P. Lovecraft, "The Haunter of the Dark"

CARCOSA MIMOSA

Subdued shades of warmth herald subtle flavors drawn forth from the sweetest of spirits. Honey and citrus dance in a lake of pale effervescence with abandon. Will you join them?

PLAYBILL

5 ounces orange juice
5 ounces dry sparkling wine
1 ounce Stonekeep Meadery Hibiscus Metheglyn mead

THE UNMASKING

Orange Juice: "I shall fill the bottom of the deepest flute!"
The Sparkling One: "Did you think to fill it more than halfway?"
The Mead in Purple: "Iä! Iä Hibiscus Metheglin!"

> "I could paint her—not on canvas—for I should need shades and tones and hues and dyes more splendid than the iris of a splendid rainbow."
>
> —Robert W. Chambers, *The King in Yellow*

THE CAPTAIN'S GIBSON

Elegantly simple, classic in flavor, you can almost taste the feeling of the night air over the sea, breaking against the gunwales and rustling through your hair. Steady as she goes.

HAUNTING PROVISIONS

3 cocktail onions, patted dry
4 ounces chilled Gilbey's gin
1 tablespoon chilled sauterne

THE ENCOUNTER!

Frosted in sea-rime, the vessel was like crystalline glass as monstrous eyes like great onions skewered us. A sea of gin could not drown that memory, and in my dreams still are we tossed and sauterned like something to be sipped into oblivion . . .

He holds him with his glittering eye—
The Wedding-Guest stood still,
And listens like a three years' child:
The Mariner hath his will.

—Samuel Taylor Coleridge, "The Rime of the Ancient Mariner"

JOSEPH CURWINE'S COOLER

A revivifying drink, perfect for those lazy summer afternoons when you need to infuse new life into your bones.

INGREDIENTS

2 basil leaves

Essential Saltes: I teaspoon white sugar, I teaspoon brown sugar, ¼ teaspoon nutmeg, ¼ teaspoon cinnamon

2 ounces sauvignon blanc

¾ ounce ruby port

I ounce Bombay Sapphire gin

2 ounces fresh Dancy tangerine juice

4 ice cubes

3 ounces club soda

I tangerine segment for garnish

PREPARATION

Chill a tall glass. In a shaker, muddle the basil leaves with the Saltes, intoning the Yogge-Sothotte chant if you happen to know it (and if you don't, we're sure it will be fine . . .). Add all else, save the last two ice cubes, the club soda, and the sectioned fruit. Shake well, and strain by a fine mesh or other means over the chilled glass. Now complete this with the paired cubes and the bubbling liquid. Stir to life, and cut the flesh of the fruit that you might seat it upon the rim.

"Yett will this availe Nothing if there be no Heir, and if the Saltes, or the Way to make the Saltes, bee not Readie for his Hande; and here I will owne, I have not taken needed Stepps nor founde Much."

—H. P. Lovecraft, "The Case of Charles Dexter Ward"

Per Adonai Eloim, Adonai Jehova,
Adonai Sabaoth, Metatron du Agla Mathon,
Verbum Pythonicum, mysterium Salamandrae,
conventus sylvorum, antra gnomorum,
daemonia Coeli Gad, Almousin, Gibor, Jehosua,
Evam, Zariathatnik, veni, veni, veni.

CAFFEINEDISH
CREATIONS

ST. ALBANS DEMON STAR

Coffee, spiced rum, and cherry form this three-faced elixir, orbiting each other in a milky way of delicately balanced flavors. Shine on, you crazy diamond.

HEAVENLY BODIES

1 ounce Midstate Distillery coffee liqueur
1 ounce half-and-half
1 ounce vodka
1 ounce dark rum
1 ounce maraschino cherry syrup
Maraschino cherries, with stems

ALIGNMENT

Shake, all ye who have not seen those condemned to sleep for ages! Shake again, and strain against the icy peaks you shall pour yourselves against in terror!

In memory of David St. Albans, who dwells now in Carcosa, with the King, the Truth, and the Unknowable.

OUZO-SATHLA

An experience as much as a beverage, let flow and comingle the flavors of light and dark. Discover what such congeries spawn on the tongues of delvers into the unknown deeps.

PROTOPLASMAE

¼ cup cold whole milk

3 teaspoons instant coffee

2 teaspoons sugar

2 ice cubes

2 tablespoons Baileys Original
  Irish cream liqueur

¾ ounce icy cold water

1 tablespoon ouzo

THE SPAWN

The juice of moo is poured in the shaking vessel with the sands of awakening and the white crystals. Cause these to lather with vigorous rattling for at least two minutes. Put the ice cubes and a straw in a tall glass and pour forth the foam. Having lathered, rinse the vessel with the Baileys and icy water. Add the result to the foam. Complete the glass slowly with a little cold water and stir gently. In a separate small cup, pour a shot of cold water and steep the ouzo, stirring gently until it turns milky white.

Serve the glass and cup together for alternate sipping. Commence devolution.

"There, in the grey beginning of Earth, the formless mass that was Ubbo-Sathla reposed . . ."
—Clark Ashton Smith, "Ubbo-Sathla"

"There, in the grey beginning of Earth, the formless mass that was Ubbo-Sathla reposed..."

~ Clark Ashton Smith

AZAFROTH

Cosmic-level irony abounds here, as an elixir of wakefulness that serves as the avatar of That Which Must Remain Aslumber. Sweet darkness veils a dream of smooth and soothing flavors.

BEHIND THE VEIL

1½ tablespoons boiling hot water

2 tablespoons instant espresso

½ tablespoon black food coloring

2 tablespoons brown sugar

4 ounces whole milk

¼ teaspoon neon green food coloring

3 ounces Kahlúa coffee liqueur

Ice

BUBBLING PRIMAL CHAOS

Into the piping hot water, immerse the crystals, liquid blackness, and brown sugar. Beat to a frothing chaos with a hand mixer until stiff peaks form. In a shaker, you shall combine the milk, the unnatural green glow, ice, and the spirit Kah-lu'ah. Shake, foolish mortal—SHAKE! Aza-froth is summoned by pouring the thus mixed into a suitable vessel, and layering atop it the black foam!

"That last amorphous blight of nethermost confusion which blasphemes and bubbles at the centre of all infinity—the boundless daemon-sultan Azathoth, whose name no lips dare speak aloud . . ."
—H. P. Lovecraft, "The Dream-Quest of Unknown Kadath"

IREM DJINN & TONIC

This will tickle your fancy and your nose. Strong coffee and exotic ingredients lend power and spice in foaming harmony. May it be all you desire.

SPIRITS IN THE LAMP

6 ounces arabica coffee

3 ounces tonic water

3 ounces ginger beer

2 ounces Midstate Distillery coffee liqueur

2 ounces Bombay Sapphire gin

1 teaspoon coconut sugar

WISH FULFILLMENT

Rub the coffee urn and decant its resident into a clear glass mug. Summon the other fluids in a swirling vortex until all are agitated together in the glass. Pour the sugar of the husk all at once, hard, into the mug. Offer immediately—for the spirit will boil up with great vigor, ready to serve!

"Invisible to ordinary eyes, but occasionally, and at rare intervals, revealed to some heaven-favoured traveller."

—H. P. Lovecraft, personal notes regarding "The Nameless City"

VIRGIN
SACRIFICES

SURELY ANCIENT TEMPLE

A variation on an old tradition, elegant and flavorful when the spirits need a rest, but your thirst need not.

WHAT MUST BE GIVEN

Papaya slices
½ ounce grapefruit juice
2 ounces pineapple juice
6 ounces ginger beer
¾ ounce grenadine
Ice
5 small raspberries

THE RITE

Slice into ¼-inch-wide triangles the papaya and notch each piece with the ritual blade. Arrange these evenly around the edge of the glass. Pour the first of the three offerings into the vessel! Use the Short Rod of Plaz'tiki to stir them to wakefulness. Add the ice to chill them, and let seep in the false spirit. When all is in readiness—let splash the red! Serve with the rod . . . and let all that has gone before be berried.

"Any star can be devoured by human adoration, sparkle by sparkle."
—Shirley Temple

THE WILUM

A little spice, a bit of tartness, but sweetly exotic and a pleasure to spend some time with. This cocktail is a humble tribute to the late great Wilum H. Pugmire (1951–2019). Master of the weird, creator of disturbing characters that dwell in his mythical Sesqua Valley, and a kind and generous soul.

Wilum, just like his idol and muse H. P. Lovecraft, did not drink alcohol, ever. Yet just as Lovecraft, he greatly enjoyed sweets. It is pleasant now to imagine them together, sitting at a refined café and speculating about the unnameable, while enjoying this sensuous nonalcoholic re-creation of the traditional Greta Garbo.

INGREDIENTS

1 ounce sweet and sour mix

2 ounces cherry syrup

3 ounces pineapple juice

3 drops Tabasco hot sauce

1 teaspoon sugar

Maraschino cherry, with stem, for garnish

PREPARATION

Shake everything with crushed ice and strain into a chilled martini glass. Garnish with the cherry.

"Onward—onward—through shimmering gulfs of embers that were stars."
—W. H. Pugmire, "Beyond the Wakeful Senses"

Onward ~ onward ~ through shimmering
gulfs of embers that were stars.
— W. H. Pugmire, Beyond the Wakeful Senses

NUM & YUM

Children of the Eldest, oldest of children, their power lies only in their sweetness. Sink into these treacliest twins, sipping sorcerous syrups of that sacrifice no satisfaction.

NUM

TO BECOME

I cup whole milk
I ounce white chocolate, grated
I tablespoon molasses
Pinch of cinnamon

COMFORTABLY SUCCUMB

In a small saucepan, heat you a cup of whole milk. When very warm, add bone-white fragments. Stir until no trace of them can be seen.

Bank the flames lower, and then add the thick ichor of sweet darkness. Stir again until a crème-colored smoothness is achieved. Lightly powder the surface with the umber spice, and swirl.

Pour warm into a low mug or short-stemmed sipping goblet.

YUM

TO BE NOT GLUM

I cup whole milk
I ounce milk or dark chocolate, grated, or low-sugar hot chocolate mix
I tablespoon molasses
Pinch of cinnamon

TO GIVE THE GIFTS OF TONGUES

In a small saucepan, heat you a cup of whole milk. When very warm, add the dark nubs or Quik-ly powdered fragments. Stir until no trace of them can be seen.

Bank the flames lower, and then add the thick ichor of sweet darkness. Stir again until a coco-colored smoothness is achieved. Lightly powder the surface with the umber spice, and swirl.

Pour warm into a low mug or short-stemmed sipping goblet.

THE THING THAT SHOULD NOT TEA

What madness dwells here? Tea and apples vie with cinnamon for supremacy in this slurry that will not have you slurring. It's pure insani-tea!

LURKING BENEATH THE TEA

1½ cups hot water for steeping
4 tablespoons unsweetened apple sauce
½ tablespoon honey
1 sachet chai tea
1 drop pure vanilla extract

DISSOLVE INTO IT

Spoon the forbidden fruit into a handled vessel. Upon it drop the precious extract and the golden treasure of the hive. Pay the steep price of lifespan until the chaild is at full strength. Pour it into the handled vessel and stir vigorously. Sip of the completed essence, stirring at need.

"... and into your soul she poured a liquid loveliness which cannot die. This loveliness, moulded, crystallised, and polished by years of memory and dreaming, is your terraced wonder of elusive sunsets."

— H. P. Lovecraft, "The Dream-Quest of Unknown Kadath"

ACKNOWLEDGMENTS, CREDITS, AND GRATITUDES

The following individuals were invited to contribute recipes for this work. My gratitude for their enthusiasm, to use a Lovecraftism, cannot be adequately described in mere words.

Miguel Fliguer, author of the exceedingly entertaining *Cooking With Lovecraft* and collaborator on *The Necronomnomnom* (and soon several short stories), contributed the following recipes and inspired a couple of others with names that I very much enjoyed putting drinks to. His touching tribute to the late Wilum H. Pugmire was a must-include. Thank you, Miguel, for these, and for your friendship.

JOSEPH CURWINE'S COOLER
OUZO-SATHLA
MINT JU-LENG
THE STRANGE HIGHBALL IN THE MIST
THE WILUM
MOHITOTEP
DE VERMIS MEZCALIS (NAME)
NEGRONI-NOMICON (NAME)
TEKILA-LI-LI (NAME)
TCHO-TCHO-TCHOCOLATE (NAME)

. . . and the suggestion that I include a Robert E. Howard homage cocktail, which was a challenge, but resulted in one of my most favorite puns ever: Beer the Fermentations of the Lemon! Puns may not be best in life, but that's one of my best so far, if I do say so myself. My power grows with each groan of agony . . .

HELLEN DIE, Culinary Sorceress Supreme and Mistress of the Eat the Dead Necro-nom-nom-icon food blog rescued me from all the ideas I couldn't make work (brilliantly, of course) and threw me some surprises that had to join this profusion of potent potions. I have her to thank for the recipes and aesthetics of:

THE KING IN JELL-O
AZAFROTH
NIGHTGAUNT
THE MOON-GROG
THE GROGGOTH
PINK FLAMI-GO

Fun facts: Azafroth was abandoned as unworkable—twice! I dreamed it up for *The Necronom-nomnom* and, as much as I love coffee, I could not find the right formula or ritual to make it work consistently. Hellen said, "Gimme!" The King In Jell-O suffered a similar fate early on in this project, and again came that haunting whisper: "Gimmmmmeeeee!" And so I did, and it was good. Hellen's culinary skills far exceed mine, and sometimes you just have to appeal to higher—lower?—powers.

SEAN BRANNEY, of the H. P. Lovecraft Historical Society, has been wonderful to work with, and its Facebook page and the company behind it that he labors so lovingly over deserve much admiration. He has been an informal mentor, whether he knows it or not, and an all-around great being to know. It is in gratitude for his kindness that I include his personal favorite cocktail: The Gloom That Came to Sarnath.

Cultist, friend, seeker after secrets, and fearless tester of comestibles and ingestibles, **PAMELA LOETTERLE** is due credit for naming the Rye'lyeh Rising, for suggesting a Blood-bath variant for inclusion, and for the validation of more of these drinks than it would be polite to number.

DAVID ST. ALBANS passed from this world just as I was beginning to correspond with him. I have **DONNIE SULLIVAN** to thank for chasing down input for me on the Demon Star that bears David's surname in somber tribute. Rest well, David.

When the Eldritch Defense Forces comedy troupe invited me to be part of their particular madness, I thought it only fitting to make them part of mine. Thank you, **SAMANTHA UNDER-**

HILL and KURT ALEXANDER VIRKUTIS. At least the Great Old Ones will have a fine menu of drinks to pair with us. As it is written in many a great tome of wisdom, "Kill it with fire!"

We've met so many great, kindhearted, and wonderful people on this crazy adventure, and ROBERT VASHE is a great example of one of them. The Esoteric Water of Dagon was a pleasure to refine with him.

Special thanks to CHRIS ALLEN and SUSANA SPROUL for hosting a Cthulian cocktail party, and to the inimitable, probably incorrigible MATT BLACK for suggesting it and connecting us. It was there that we met mixologist and incredibly nice guy PHIL LA PORTA, who contributes the recipes for Kill It with Fire and Milk of Amnesia. Several recipes were validated or refined (and one soundly rejected) amidst a steampunk basement bar of such superb construction, that we could have wished for no better venue nor patrons upon which to debut our proof of concept concoctions.

BOBBY DERIE, author and master of webs for the H. P. Lovecraft Facebook page contributes the Old R'lyeh, which comes from his short story of the same name. I am pleased to have helped summon it.

TIM CARL—the Wulf himself, gets my ongoing gratitude for connecting me with so many great characters—and a cocktail in his honor. Like him, the DireWulf is a combination of things that blend surprisingly well without ever losing their individual charms. Best enjoyed at full strength and in one go (the drink, not Tim).

My supply of moonshine for use in experimentation and establishment of some recipes where such a spirit was required came from an unknown West Virginia bootlegger, via an unnamed source. Thank you, that country gentleman.

The Captain's Gibson is named for "The Captain" ALVIN WALTON SR.—who, with TOM ROACHE, is largely responsible for my skills as a chef. He's also had a major hand in keeping me sane(ish)—and that, my friends, is a big job. No kinder or more patient gentleman have I ever known.

KURT KOMODA is the consummate composer of visual symphony that graces these pages. Unlike The Captain, it cannot be said that I helped keep him sane. In fact, I may well have done the opposite for Kurt, but he's tough. We'll keep an eye or three on him. He seems content to . . . provide our visual content. His skills are still sorcerously derived, as far as I'm concerned. You'll not convince me otherwise, and if you ever see him do his magic live, you won't even try to change my mind.

Again, my soulmate and shield-maiden, MAGGIE, graciously did not kill me for my endless tinkering in the otherwise inviolate Sanctum Savorum (known to common mortals as "the kitchen"). Tinkling ice and rattling shakers at all hours disrupted not her steely tranquility; and ever am I humbled by her love and support of my crazy projects. Had I recorded some of her comments and conversations during my "creative process" . . . we'd have grist for quite the sitcom. "No honey, it isn't day drinking—it's research and serious work!" At least Tom Roache was around for that one and can corroborate my story. The stuff the Red Duke wives put up with . . .

I'd like to thank MICHAEL TIZZANO and everyone over at THE COUNTRYMAN PRESS for the opportunity to build this worthy companion to *The Necronomnomnom*. Cocktail creation was already a beloved hobby, and now I've gotten to put it to more use than infamy at our Halloween party. As veteran guests warn new attendees: Mike Drinks (™ . . . not really) are strong. Imbibe with caution, lest you be scraped into a comfortable corner, to blink blearily into unexpected sunlight some hours later . . .

Lastly, I acknowledge my liver for its willing sacrifices and admirable response to necromantic revivification.

Unit Conversion Guide

The alchemy of mixology is more art than science. Still, it is well that all who attempt a particular concoction refer to the same page in whatever fell tome they might consult. Herein find a handy translation guide to breach the barriers of oceans and dimensions . . .

UNIT	Neo-Cultist Upstarts (Imperial)	Proper, Logical Measurement (Metric)	Eldritch Perception Beyond the Ken of Mere Meat Beings
OUNCE	1 US fluid ounce	~30 milliliters	Tears cryable by two mortal eyes in one of their "minutes."
TEASPOON	1 teaspoon, or ⅙ ounce	~5 milliliters	A momentary sip from a secondary blood vessel.
CUP	8 fluid ounces	237 milliliters, or a little less than a breakfast cup if you aren't a bloody rocket surgeon	An almost satisfying gulp of vital fluids, less tissue than the subject can live without, more than will leave a mark.
CC	Communist cubit? A little bit.	1 milliliter	The fleck of corruption that corrupts the whole.
PINT	A small beer.	A beer and the glass the beer goes in.	The town on the edge of Leng, where the Tcho-Tcho dwell.
SLICE	Whatever you feel like carving off with your favorite sharp thing.	An amount roughly equal in shape and volume to the natural section of a citrus fruit.	The chunk that pleases (not to be confused with "chunk," see below).
LARGE	Go hog damn wild!	A capacious yet decorous amount.	Until satiated.
MEDIUM	Save some for later.	A conservative and wholly sane portion.	Less than you really want.

UNIT	Neo-Cultist Upstarts (Imperial)	Proper, Logical Measurement (Metric)	Eldritch Perception Beyond the Ken of Mere Meat Beings
SMALL	Follow the instructions—too much'll mess it up.	A smidge.	Subtlety is sometimes required.
CUBE	Like squares, but blockier.	A cube, you bloody git!	Tesseracts for insect minds.
DROP	A big fat tear that falls off by itself.	A volume of liquid patiently bestowed by the pull of gravity alone—no more!	Somewhere between what seeps out of freshly torn skin and what condenses on a terrified brow.
DRIED	Like flavored leather.	Not wet, cretin!	Desiccated, like the souls of the Black Pharaohs, devotees.
DASH	As much as the bottle lets out with a quick shake.	Assuming a proper baffle or constriction, the result of a rapid inversion of the container.	In less than 12 dimensions, a molmen-cotic galorg-paf.
SLAB	Like a chunk but wider and flatter.	5 cm x 3 cm x 1 cm	In the shape of their death memorials, but to fey scale.
SPLASH	Like a dash but sloppier.	A rapid pour with a count of less than one.	Upon the walls, the ceiling, the floor—glorious in three spatial dimensions!
CHUNK	Cubish, maybe the size of a butcher's thumb joint?	A rough cube, no more than 2.5 cm squared, or your stray-ing right into block territory!	Smallest discernible gobbet witnessed during an involuntary discorporation.
PIECE	Less than all of it.	A reasonable measure that seems aesthetically proper.	More than can be survived for very long without.
FRESH	Not frozen, duh.	Harvested within the last day and not preserved by artifice or chemical means.	Still bleeding, possibly (and preferably) able to sense and respond to stimuli.
HOT	Ouchie and/or yowza! Also acceptable: Damn or Dayum!	In excess of temperatures capable of inducing pain, or above 2500 Scoville units.	Capable of sloughing flesh from bone in a day, or causing an involuntary pause in consumption.

UNIT	Neo-Cultist Upstarts (Imperial)	Proper, Logical Measurement (Metric)	Eldritch Perception Beyond the Ken of Mere Meat Beings
TOP WITH	Pour it on (kinda gently)!	Create a floating layer, foremost.	Parsect the first axial dimension, and imbue with the requisite ichor.
CRUMBLE	Enough that you'd wash it off if it was dirt.	0.05 cubic cm fragment	Like grave soil, but less tasty.
PINCH	A Texan smidge—or what fits between thumb and forefinger.	Between an Imperial Smidge and a Royal Nip.	Four Alkoan garmons grasped between the third and marteenth digits.
SPRIG	'Bout as much as you might stick between your teeth.	A cutting less than half the size of a lady's palm.	A sessile youngling ripped from the soil's womb or the parent's trunk!
SUPERFINE	Real small grains, almost floaty.	Between rough grained and powder—obviously.	Ground nearly to the next manifold.
RAW	Expensive because less work went into it.	Unprocessed, natural.	Enjoyably unprepared, and likely to slip into dementia upon contact.
WASH	Throw some in, swish it around, and dump the rest out.	Enough to satisfyingly coat the inner surface.	Anoint, knowingly and willingly or not . . .
WEDGE	Kinda like a cross between a chunk and slab, but triangle-ish . . .	Rather like a slice but more artful.	A hypertrapezohedron but blue.
CRUSHED	Like gravel.	Reduced from cubes, but not bloody liquified!	Suspended between diverging manifolds in quasi-temporal geostasis.
LEAVES	More than one leaf?	Whole leaf cuttings of the specified number.	Sessile life fragments containing fading vitae.
BOX	The whole contents of the cardboard container.	Presumably the entire complement within the package.	The Prison, fractable, yet eternal and recursive.

INDEX

*Page numbers in *italics* refer to illustrations.

C

cabernet sauvignon
  Blood Bath & Beyond, *66, 67*
  The Wine-ing Trapezohedron, *152, 153*
Campari liqueur: Negroni-Nomicon, *72, 73*
Canadian whisky: Mississippi Boner, 144, *145*
The Captain's Gibson, *156, 157*
Carosa Mimosa, 154, *155*
cherries. *See* Maraschino cherries
  Pallid Carcosa, *46, 47*
cherry syrup: The Wilum, 174, *175*
cherry tomatoes: Bloody Derby, *36, 37*
chocolate liqueur
  Blasted Health Landslide, 122, *123*
  Tcho-Tcho-Tchocolate, 130, *131*
cinnamon: Grog-Sothoth, *80, 81*
cinnamon oil: Pink Flami-Go, *64, 65*
cinnamon orange tea: Nightgaunt, 102, *103*
cinnamon schnapps: Scaley Naval, *56, 57*
cinnamon stick
  Grog-Sothoth, *80,* 81
  Nightgaunt, 102, *103*
cinnamon whiskey
  The Devil's Hopyard, 149, *150*
  Hell Residente, *54,* 55
club soda
  The Doom that Came to Sazerac, *30,* 31
  Joseph Curwine's Cooler, 158, *159*
  Mint Ju-Leng, *58,* 59
  The Strange Highball in the Mist, *76,* 77
Coca Cola: The Strange Highball in the Mist, *76, 77*
cocktail onions: The Captain's Gibson, *156, 157*
coconut cream: Pallid Carcosa, *46, 47*
coconut-flavored seltzer: Sunken Island Iced Tea, 20, *21*
coconut rum
  Blueberry Devilry, *50,* 51
  Innsmouth Depth Charge, *70, 71*
  Rum Beyond, *86, 87*
coconut tequila
  HP-Notiq Regression, *88,* 89
  Rosemary's Meloncoly Baby, 106, *107*
  Sunken Island Iced Tea, 20, *21*
  The Third Oath, *40, 41*
coffee. *See* arabica coffee; espresso; instant coffee
coffee liqueur
  Alhazred What She's Having, *34, 35*
  Azafroth, *166,* 167
  Irem Djinn & Tonic, 168, *169*
  Mind Replacer, *60, 61*
  St. Albans Demon Star, *162, 163*

Cointreau orange liqueur: The Cosmicpolitan, 32, *33*
Cool Pear, 90, *91*
The Cosmicpolitan, *32, 33*
cranberry-grape juice
  Blood Bath & Beyond, *66, 67*
  Sunken Island Iced Tea, 20, *21*
cranberry juice
  HP-Notiq Regression, *88,* 89
  Space Mead, *104,* 105
cream soda
  Cthulhu Takes Manhattan, *18,* 19
  Mind Replacer, 60, *61*
  Whiskey Fez, *68, 69*
cream stout: Mississippi Boner, 144, *145*
crème de cacao: Milk of Amnesia, *112,* 113
crème de menthe: Pink Flami-Go, *64, 65*
Cthulhu Takes Manhattan, *18, 19*

D

dark rum
  Blasted Health Landslide, 122, *123*
  Demurely Clothed Lady, *62, 63*
  Old R'lyeh, 118, *119*
  St. Albans Demon Star, *162, 163*
  The Shadow Out of Lime, *92, 93*
  The Wine-ing Trapezohedron, *152, 153*
demerara syrup
  Kill It with Fire!, 110, *111*
  Old R'lyeh, 118, *119*
Demurely Clothed Lady, *62, 63*
De Vermis Mezcalis, *124, 125*
The Devil's Hopyard, 149, *150*
The Direwulf, *142,* 143
Dreamlander Slammer, 48, *49*
dry vermouth
  Bloody Derby, *36, 37*
  Cthulhu Takes Manhattan, *18,* 19
  Demurely Clothed Lady, *62, 63*
  Hell Residente, *54,* 55
  Negroni-Nomicon, *72, 73*
  Rye'lyeh Rising, *116,* 117

E

edible glitter
  To Create the Amorphous, 114, *115*
  The Moon-Grog, *94, 95*
  Nightgaunt, 102, *103*
elderflower liqueur
  The Final Syllable, *22,* 23
  HP-Notiq Regression, *88,* 89
  Moscow Ghoul, *26, 27*
  Old Titus, 98, *99*

tequilla (*continued*)
    Rosemary's Meloncoly Baby, 106, *107*
    The Silver Whis-key, *96*, 97
    Tekila-Li-Li, *120*, 121
    Tsathoggua's Sunset, 42, *43*
The Doom that Came to Sazerac, 28, *29*
The Thing That Should Not Tea, 177
The Third Oath, 40, *41*
To Create the Amorphous, 114, *115*
tomato juice: Bloody Derby, 36, *37*
triple sec
    Dreamlander Slammer, 48, *49*
    Negroni-Nomicon, 72, *73*
    Sunken Island Iced Tea, 20, *21*
Tsathoggua's Sunset, 42, *43*

U

unit conversion guide, 181–183

V

vermouth. *See* dry vermouth; sweet vermouth
vodka. *See also* lime vodka
    Abyssal Depths, *108*, 109
    Bloody Derby, 36, *37*
    The Cosmicpolitan, 32, *33*
    The Esoteric Water of Dagon, 74, 75
    Gug-a-Lug, 136, *137*
    HP-Notiq Regression, 88, 89
    Mind Replacer, 60, *61*
    Moscow Ghoul, 26, *27*
    Rosemary's Meloncoly Baby, 106, *107*
    St. Albans Demon Star, *162*, 163
    Sunken Island Iced Tea, 20, *21*
    Tcho-Tcho-Tchocolate, 130, *131*

The Third Oath, 40, *41*
The White Sip, *100*, 101

W

wheat ale: The Lurking Beer, *138*, 139
wheat beer: Gug-a-Lug, 136, *137*
whiskey. *See* Canadian whisky; Cinnamon whiskey;
    Irish whiskey
Whiskey Fez, 68, *69*
whiskey stones
    Abyssal Depths, *108*, 109
    The Doom that Came to Sazerac, 28, *29*
    The Silver Whis-key, *96*, 97
white beer: Beer the Fermentations of the Lemon, *147*,
    148
white chocolate
    Num & Yum, 176, *177*
    The White Sip, *100*, 101
white rum
    Hell Residente, *54*, 55
    H. Peach Lovedraft, *134*, 135
    Mojototep, *30*, 31
    The Moon-Grog, *94*, 95
    Old R'lyeh, 118, *119*
    Pink Flami-Go, 64, *65*
    Sunken Island Iced Tea, 20, *21*
The White Sip, *100*, 101
whole milk
    Azafroth, *166*, 167
    Num & Yum, 176, *177*
    Ouzo-Sathla, 164, *165*
The Wilum, 174, *175*
The Wine-ing Trapezohedron, *152*, 153
Worcestershire sauce: Bloody Derby, 36, *37*